Page Turners

Second Chances

Sue Leather

Series Editors:
Rob Waring and Sue Leather

Series Story Consultant: Julian Thomlinson

NATIONAL GEOGRAPHIC LEARNING | CENGAGE Learning

Australia • Brazil • Japan • Korea • Mexico • Singapore • Spain • United Kingdom • United States

NATIONAL GEOGRAPHIC LEARNING | CENGAGE Learning

Page Turners Reading Library

Second Chances
Sue Leather

Publisher: Andrew Robinson

Executive Editor: Sean Bermingham

Development Editor:
Charlotte Sharman

Associate Development Editor:
Sarah Tan

Editorial Assistant: Vivian Chua

Director of Global Marketing:
Ian Martin

Senior Content Project Manager:
Tan Jin Hock

Manufacturing Planner:
Mary Beth Hennebury

Contributor: Jessie Chew

Layout Design and Illustrations:
Redbean Design Pte Ltd

Cover Illustration: Eric Foenander

ISBN-13: 978-1-4240-4642-3

ISBN-10: 1-4240-4642-4

National Geographic Learning
20 Channel Center Street
Boston, Massachusetts 02210
USA

Cengage Learning is a leading provider of customized learning solutions with office locations around the globe, including Singapore, the United Kingdom, Australia, Mexico, Brazil, and Japan. Locate your local office at:
international.cengage.com/region

Cengage Learning products are represented in Canada by Nelson Education, Ltd.

Visit National Geographic Learning online at **NGL.Cengage.com**

Visit our corporate website at **www.cengage.com**

Printed in the United States of America
1 2 3 4 5 6 7 – 17 16 15 14 13

Contents

Background Reading

People in the story

Mary Diaz
Mary is a communications student at Brenton College. She is in her early 20s.

Katy Burns
Katy is a media studies student, and a friend and roommate of Mary's.

John Pearson
John is a businessman from London and Mary's biological father. He is in his early 40s.

This story is set in Brenton College, a fictional place in Seattle, USA; and in London, England.

Chapter 1

Chocolates

"Are you really sure you want me to stay, Mary?" Katy asked. "I can go to soccer practice a little early, you know."

Mary looked at her friend. "I told you, Katy," she said, "I want you to be with me when he comes." She looked at the clock on the wall of Ben's Café. "I want to see what he wants."

"Well . . ."

"I mean, after all this time. It's a little strange, isn't it?" Mary said, not for the first time that afternoon. "Coming to Brenton twenty years after he left my mom?" She took a drink of her coffee.

"I guess so," said Katy. "But it's exciting!"

"Exciting?" Mary couldn't stop moving. She took the letter from her father out of her pocket again, and started reading. *"I'm in Seattle for a few days on business and I think it's a good chance for us to meet,"* she read. She turned to Katy. "Why now?"

"You've read that about ten times," laughed Katy. "He'll be here very soon and you can ask him."

Just then, the door of Ben's Café opened, and a tall, slim man walked in. He had a smile on his face and a box of chocolates in his hand.

"Mary," said the man, walking to the table where Mary and Katy sat. "I'm John. I'm really happy to meet you." He spoke with a British accent. "You look just like the photograph you sent." He held out the chocolates.

"Umm . . . yeah," she said, feeling like she had no words suddenly. She looked at the chocolates.

"I hope you like chocolates . . . ?" he said.

"Sure," she said.

Mary looked up at the tall man in the smart business suit. How could she be so different from him? she asked herself. How could he be so different from *her*? For one thing, he was so . . . well, *smart,* in his suit and tie. Everyone told her she always looked untidy. Now her father was here, she couldn't speak. She felt uncomfortable.

John moved toward her as if he wanted to hug her, but she moved away quickly.

"Is it OK if I sit down?" he asked.

"Oh, yeah, sure," she said.

"Katy, my . . . umm . . . John," Mary said. John and Katy shook hands and John sat down at the little table.

"Like some coffee?" asked Katy. "We're . . . umm . . ." John looked at their cups and nodded. Katy went to get coffee for him.

"Nice place," John said, looking round the café. "It wasn't here when I studied at Brenton."

"It's OK, I guess," said Mary. She looked round, too. It was afternoon and there were only two other students in the café. They were sitting quietly, drinking coffee and reading.

Katy came back and put the coffee down in front of him. The three of them talked about the weather and changes in Brenton for a few moments.

"It looks very different," said John. "The town is really busy now. And the college, well, it's bigger than when I was here." He took a drink of his coffee.

"Did you see the new library?" Katy asked. "It's a really great building."

"No. I just came to see Mary," he said. "It's a short visit." He looked at Mary and added, "I leave for London early tomorrow."

Nobody spoke for a moment or two. Katy finished her coffee then started to put her jacket on. Mary looked at her.

Katy stood up. "Well, I'll leave you two now. I really have to go," she said, speaking to John and not looking at Mary. "Sorry—soccer practice. Nice to meet you. See you later, Mary!"

"But . . ." Mary started, but Katy was gone.

John smiled at Mary. Mary drank her coffee. They didn't speak for a few moments.

"Mary . . ." he started.

"Coffee OK?" she asked.

"Great," he said.

A few more moments of quiet.

"Thanks for seeing me," he said. "I didn't know if . . ."

"Sure," said Mary, but she didn't smile.

The café seemed to go quiet. The only sound was the tick-tock of the clock.

"I know this is difficult," John said after a while. "The thing is, Mary, I know how you must feel . . ."

"Really?"

"I mean, a little," John said. "I know that nothing can change what happened, but I want another chance. I want us to get to know each other." He held his hands tightly together. Mary saw his expensive gold watch.

"Why?" she asked.

"Because I'm your father," he said quietly.

Mary didn't reply. It was quiet for a moment or two as she just looked at the man in front of her. A bird sang outside. One of the students in the café turned a page of his book.

"I know Isabel died last year and I'm really sorry. I . . ."

Mary gave him a look that said, "Don't talk about Mom."

"Listen, Mary," John said quietly, "I can guess how you feel about me, but I want to show you I'm not a bad man. I'm . . ."

"Sorry?" asked Mary. "You're sorry?"

John didn't answer, but put his hand into the inside pocket of his jacket. He brought out a check and put it on the table in front of Mary.

"Look, this is a very quick visit to Seattle for me. It's all business. I have to go soon, but here's a check," he said. "It's Spring Break the week after next. Come to London and stay with me. Bring someone. Anyone you want. I know you have a lot of questions. We can really get to know each other."

A few moments later, John Pearson was gone. Mary sat looking at enough money for two first-class tickets to London, England.

Chapter 2

Arrivals

"London? But that's wonderful!" Katy said.

"Is it?" Mary held out the box of chocolates and Katy took one.

"Well, I . . . I mean, why not?"

"Let me tell you, Katy," said Mary, turning round to face her friend. "He leaves Mom twenty years ago. He never even sees me! He sends a letter or two. Then suddenly he's here, saying he's sorry and asking me to go to London 'to get to know him better.' How would *you* feel?"

"Well, I know what you mean," Katy said, "but at least he's open with you."

"You just want a trip to London!"

Katy smiled. "Well, it will be nice," she said. "But think about it. You have no mom or dad now. Don't you think you need someone?"

Mary's stepdad, Larry Diaz, died five years ago, and her mom, Isabel, died just last year.

"I have Aunt Lucy," Mary said. Lucy was Mary's

mother's sister. She was helping Mary get through college now that her mom and stepdad were gone.

"I know," said Katy. "But you're not that close to her. You *know* you aren't."

It was true. Lucy was nice, but she was very different from Isabel—and from Mary. Mary missed her mother every day.

Katy went on. "And you know it's not easy for you, studying and working."

Mary worked in a café in Brenton most days to help pay for college. It was difficult to do both.

"I don't know, Katy," said Mary. "I've hated this man all my life. He left Mom when I wasn't even born. Mom and me, well . . . we didn't have much. I grew up poor. I can't suddenly have good feelings for him." She looked across the dorm room at Katy.

"I know, Mary," Katy said. "I understand. Really, I do. I'm just saying maybe you should give him a chance. I mean, do you really know the full story about him?"

"What's to know?" Mary asked, her eyes angry. "He left his wife who was having a baby!"

Katy put up her hands and said, "OK, OK. I don't know. Why not ask your Aunt Lucy what she thinks?"

Mary called her Aunt Lucy and told her all about the meeting with John Pearson. Lucy agreed with Katy. It wasn't a bad idea, she thought, for Mary to get to know her father. "You know," Lucy said, "I think getting to know him is a very good idea. You're not that different from him."

"Oh *really*?!"

"Yes, really," Lucy smiled. "I think you'll understand yourself better if you get to know him." Anyway, Lucy said, what did Mary have to lose?

Mary wasn't so sure. But ten days later, Mary and Katy went to Seattle to get on a plane to London.

◇◇◇

"How was the flight?" John Pearson was smiling widely as he walked up to Mary and Katy at the Arrivals hall in Heathrow Airport.

"Wonderful!" said Katy. "We had a lot of fun. The food was great, and there were lots of movies . . . and the seats were so comfortable . . ."

"Did you enjoy it, Mary?" asked her father.

"It was OK," said Mary. She didn't look so happy.

"Well, good. Here, let me get someone to help you with those bags." John called someone who put their bags onto a cart and pushed it toward the door.

They all walked out of the airport building and past a line of black taxis. "Over here," John said.

They walked across the road toward a very large gray car. As they went toward it, the driver, wearing a suit, got out and ran to them to help with their bags. Mary and Katy looked at the big car.

"Wow!" said Katy.

John Pearson smiled.

"It's . . . wonderful!" said Katy.

"Well, I . . ." Mary couldn't speak. Her head was full of thoughts, feelings, and questions. But she told herself just to wait and see. *Give him a chance,* Aunt Lucy said, and Mary was trying.

Katy talked a lot as they sat back in the comfortable black leather seats of the car and drove into London.

"I think you'll both love London," said John Pearson. "I live in Mayfair, right in the center of the city." He went on talking about London and all the things they could see and do there.

After a while, John stopped talking and Mary closed her eyes. When she opened them again, they were in the city. She looked out of the window. How different it all looked from Brenton, even Seattle. Most of the streets were narrow, and everywhere

was full of people. *London.* She said the name to herself a few times in her head. It was her first time in Europe. Now she was here, she felt some excitement. They drove through downtown, or the center of the city as John called it. She saw some buildings she'd seen in books or on the Internet. There were the Houses of Parliament, Big Ben, the River Thames . . .

"Look!" Katy shouted out suddenly. "There's Buckingham Palace!" They looked out at the big palace as they went round in front of it and down the wide street in front of it. "Oh, I feel just like the Queen of England!" said Katy. Mary looked at her and laughed.

"Don't worry," said John, "you'll have lots of time to look at everything. First, we'll get you home and you can have a shower and a rest. You must be very tired after that flight."

A few minutes later, they drove down a street called Piccadilly, then down a side street. They stopped outside a beautiful old building. The driver left them, and another man in his forties came out of the building and took their bags. "Mary, Katy," said Mary's father. "This is Harry." They said hello, and Harry went upstairs with the bags.

"He helps around the house." John explained.

“You mean, a servant?” asked Mary.

“Well, I don’t see him that way,” said John. “He just helps with everything. He’s a very good cook, too. You’ll see.”

The three of them went up to the top floor in the elevator. Then, John opened a door with the number 1 on it.

“Welcome!” he said. Mary and Katy walked into what Mary thought was the biggest, most beautiful apartment in the world.

Chapter 3

The sights

"Some coffee, Mary?" John Pearson said.

"Thanks," said Mary. "It smells good." She sat down at the table and took the cup of coffee. It was eight o'clock in the morning on the fourth day of their visit. Katy was already eating breakfast with John. Through the large window behind the table, Mary could see London. It was a beautiful morning.

"So how are you enjoying the city?" John asked them as Mary sat down.

"I love it!" said Katy.

"It's a great city," Mary agreed. "Very nice."

"Very nice, eh?" said John, laughing. "Well, maybe you could come and live here and enjoy it every day?" He looked carefully at Mary as he spoke.

Mary didn't answer. The room was quiet for a moment.

"How was Hyde Park yesterday?" John asked.

"Great," Mary said.

"What did you do in the afternoon?"

"We went shopping in Kensington," Mary said.

"Did you buy anything nice?" asked John.

"She bought some shoes," Katy said before Mary could speak. "As usual!" She laughed.

The two of them were having a good time. John Pearson's apartment was beautiful and very comfortable. The girls each had their own bedroom and a large bathroom. His driver, Charles, was always ready to take them anywhere in London, and Harry was at home to look after them. "This is like a dream!" Katy said more than once. But Mary was uncomfortable. She was uncomfortable with the luxurious apartment and all the money John had. And her father was busy, and it never seemed that he wanted to talk to her. Why didn't he say something? *After all,* she kept thinking, *he was the one who left us!*

"What color?" John Pearson asked.

"Color?"

"The shoes."

"Red," Mary said. She loved bright colors. "I'll show them to you later."

Just then Harry came in and asked Mary what she wanted for breakfast. He went through a long list as he did every day.

"Try the eggs and bacon today," said Katy. "They're delicious."

"I . . . umm . . . OK," said Mary. "Eggs and bacon would be nice."

Harry walked off toward the kitchen.

"What are you going to do today?" asked John.

"We want to go on the river, I think," said Mary. "Then later Katy is going to see a friend of her mom's who lives here. So I'll be alone." She looked at her father.

"Maybe you and I can do something together?" said John, but then, he put his hand to his head. "Oh, no! Sorry, Mary," he said. "I just remembered I have a really important meeting all day today. I won't be back until this evening. But we'll do that—maybe Thursday? Let's do it Thursday. That's a great idea, don't you think?" He smiled.

"Maybe," said Mary, turning away from her father.

Just then John's phone rang. He answered it, listened, and said, "Yes, OK, I'll be there in twenty minutes." Then he got up quickly and took his jacket. "Well, I have to go now," he said, "but the car is waiting for you. Just tell Charles where you want to go as usual. I'll be back this evening. If you want anything, anything at all, just ask Harry." He smiled again at Mary, but she wasn't looking at him. "OK, then . . ." he said. And with that, John Pearson left.

◇◇◇

"My own bathroom!" Katy said. Mary and Katy were in the back of the car, going toward the River Thames for their trip. "I can't believe those towels.

They're so soft!"

Mary looked out of the window at the busy streets. *We can get to know each other,* her father had said. *How? When?* she asked herself. It was four days now. Her father was always at work, always busy. She wanted him to speak to her, to make time for her. She wanted to know why he left her mom and her.

"And the bath—it's like a swimming pool! Don't you like it?" Katy just talked on.

"It's OK," said Mary.

"OK?"

"Yes. OK!"

"What's wrong with you, Mary?" asked Katy. "This is wonderful! Your father is really really rich and really great, and you act, like . . . well, like you don't care."

"Why should I care?" Mary asked, suddenly angry. "Just please stop going on about towels and baths. So he's rich. So what?"

"Well . . . I . . ."

"OK, he has money and he gives me things. But does he speak to me? Does he tell me why he's never wanted to know me until now? Does he tell me why he left Mom?" Mary's voice got louder.

Katy closed the window behind Charles in the car and looked at Mary seriously. "Listen, that's not fair, Mary.

This morning he said you could talk Thursday, and you just turned away. I saw you! I think he's really trying. He's busy, Mary. But I'm sure . . ."

"Oh, you're sure, are you?"

"I can't understand you," said Katy. "You have a really rich father with a wonderful house in London, who's always giving you things, and he wants you to come and live here."

"Why do you think that?" Mary asked.

"He said so this morning," Katy replied softly. "I mean, how wonderful for you! You'll have everything."

"You don't understand, do you?" Mary looked right into Katy's eyes. "I don't want things, I don't want everything. I want him to know what he did. I want him to know that he can't just do that, and then come back into my life like nothing happened. I want him to say sorry! I . . . aagh . . . why am I talking to you?"

Mary opened the window behind the driver. "Charles, stop the car, please. I want to get out." Mary looked at Katy as the car started to stop. "I'm going back to the apartment. I'll see you tonight."

"But I thought you wanted to go on the river?" Katy looked like she wanted to cry.

"Well, I don't!" Mary opened the door of the car, got out and walked quickly down the street.

Chapter 4

The past

At eight o'clock that evening, Mary was in the apartment, waiting for her father. She was still angry, but that afternoon she'd thought about what Katy said. Was her friend right? Mary was upset because her father hadn't spoken to her, but what about her? Maybe *she* needed to talk first, she thought.

Mary heard the door of the apartment open.

"Hello?" It was John Pearson's voice. "Is anyone there?"

Mary walked out of her room and stood in front of her father.

"Why did you leave Mom?" Mary asked. She didn't mean to start like that, but it just came out.

"I . . . umm . . . Let's sit down, Mary," he said.

"Why?" Mary asked again. She didn't smile.

John took his jacket off and moved toward the living room.

But Mary went on. Her voice was hard. "This is all a lot for me to understand," she said. She looked around the room. "I didn't grow up with . . . with all this. You're rich, really. I mean, you have lots of things.

But Mom . . . well, do you know how hard it was for us when I was a child? Mom worked seven days a week. Why didn't you help us then?"

"I know, Mary . . . I do understand."

"It was hard for me growing up. I think I need to know why you left Mom—and me."

John sat down in an armchair in the beautiful living room with its Italian furniture. Outside, the lights of London shone against a black sky.

"I was young—your age. I was studying Business at Brenton College," he started. "I met Isabel . . . your mother . . . she was a waitress. You know, at a café in Brenton. She was beautiful—just like you. We met and we fell in love." He smiled. "It was crazy," he said. "We were so much in love. We ran away and got married. It was, you know . . . crazy."

Mary didn't speak, but sat down on the sofa.

"We . . . well, we got married. Then Isabel got pregnant—with you."

"And you left," Mary said.

"I . . . it wasn't you, Mary," said John seriously. "I want you to understand that. "

"So what was it?" asked Mary.

"Isabel and I started to fight. I guess you can say we fell out of love. We both knew it wasn't going to work.

"And you just . . . left?"

"I know it doesn't look good, Mary," John said, taking a drink, "but, yes, I left."

He went on. "I tried to come back . . . to see you many times," John said. "But Isabel got married again later—to Larry. He didn't want me to see her, or you. I tried—really, I tried to see you when you were little, but I could never . . ." John's voice became very weak and he looked away from Mary.

"So why now?" asked Mary. Her voice was still hard.

"I've felt bad for a long time," he said. "I thought about you every day. I wanted to find you. And then I heard that Isabel died. I knew it was time to do something, to find you while you're still young." He smiled sadly. "And while I'm still young."

He looked into his glass for a moment, and then went on. "It was easy to find you. You have Larry's name—Diaz," he said. "I really knew I had to meet you, talk to you. It was time."

"Time? Do you know what it was like for me as a child? Knowing that my father didn't want me?" Mary said. She jumped up from the sofa, and stood looking at him.

"You didn't want me," she said again.

"It's not true that I didn't want you. It was my mistake

and I'm sorry, Mary, really I am," John said. "But I *want* to be a father to you. I want to have you in my life. I have money, and the business is going well." His voice went quiet. "But something's missing, Mary. *You're* missing. I want to do the right thing . . . to get to know you. And it would be a good life for you . . ."

Mary turned on her father, suddenly very angry. "What?! Let me understand this. After twenty years you come into my life and think everything's OK? Suddenly? You want me to leave my life and come to live in London with you?"

"I just thought . . ."

"Just like that?" She hit the table hard.

"I'm asking for a second chance, Mary," John said quietly.

"Second chance?" Mary cried, looking at him in the eyes. Then she turned and ran out of the room and to her bedroom.

Chapter 5

The future

"Mary?"

It was Katy. It was eleven o'clock at night and Katy was back from visiting her mom's friend.

"Mary, let me in."

"Go away!"

"Come on, Mary," Katy said. "I can hear you crying in there. I'm not going to go away."

A few moments later Mary opened her bedroom door and let Katy in. Mary's face was wet and her eyes were red.

"What . . . what happened?" Katy asked as they sat down on Mary's bed. Katy's voice was soft and she touched Mary's arm.

"Oh, nothing," Mary said, turning her face away.

"It doesn't look like nothing," Katy said. "Come on, tell me what it is."

Still crying, Mary told her all about the talk with her father. "He just doesn't understand," she said at last. "I hate him."

"Do you? Do you really?" Katy asked. "Listen, I know it's difficult, Mary, but I think maybe you need to give him a second chance."

"Why?"

"Because everyone needs a second chance," Katy said. "Look at you!" She smiled.

"Me?"

"You're always angry with him—and with me," Katy laughed. "Every time I talk to you, you bite my head off!"

Mary looked at her friend. "Really?"

"Really!"

"I didn't . . . I'm sorry, Katy, I just . . . all this . . ."

"I know," Katy said, smiling at her friend. "I know that it's difficult for you."

Nobody spoke for a moment.

Then Katy went on. "Listen, maybe your dad made a mistake. Maybe it was a big mistake. Who knows? Things happen. It was a long time ago. The important thing is he wants to know you *now.* He wants to be a part of your life. And I, for one, think he's a very nice man!" Katy laughed. "It's great that he's your dad."

"Well, I . . ."

"And it's not just for him, Mary," Katy said. "It's for you, too."

"I don't know what you mean."

"I think you do, Mary," Katy said. "You need to be happy too. Look at yourself. Your mom and stepdad are gone now, he's your only family really. You *need* your father. *You* need him in your life. You need him just as much as he needs you."

◇◇◇

The next morning, Mary walked into the dining room. Katy was still in her bedroom. John was at the breakfast table, reading a newspaper.

"Mary!" John put the newspaper down and got up.

"I have something to say," Mary said. "I thought about it . . ."

Her father looked at her with a question in his eyes.

"I want to say sorry about last night," she said.

"No," said her father. "I understand. Really. This isn't easy."

She went on. "I don't think it's a good idea for me to come here . . . to London, to live I mean. I want to finish with college and . . ."

"Oh," John said. He looked sad. "Well, I don't want you to stop going to college. I just thought you could do that here."

"Let me finish," Mary said, holding up her hand. "But I think I do want to get to know you, to have you in my life . . ." She stopped for a moment. "We can, you know . . . visit. You can come to Brenton . . ."

Her father suddenly smiled. He moved toward her, "And you can come here," he said.

"We can get to know each other little by little," she said.

"That will be wonderful, Mary!"

Mary smiled too. "Yes, it will," she said. "I . . . I was angry about everything before . . ."

"I understand, Mary."

"But now I understand that you didn't really want to hurt me," Mary went on.

"No, I didn't," her father said. "I never wanted to hurt you." He held out his arms.

For the first time, Mary didn't feel angry at her father. And for the first time she hugged him.

Review

A. Match the characters in the story to their descriptions.

Mary	Katy	John	Harry	Lucy	Isabel

1. ___________ is Mary's aunt.
2. ___________ was married to John Pearson.
3. ___________ is Mary's real father.
4. ___________ helps John in his home.
5. ___________ is John's daughter.
6. ___________ is Mary's best friend.

B. Read each statement and circle whether it is true (T) or false (F).

1. John Pearson is a rich businessman. T / F
2. Mary thought that John did not want to be her father. T / F
3. Katy enjoyed the trip to London more than Mary. T / F
4. John gave Mary some money for airline tickets. T / F
5. Katy suggested Mary stop hating her father. T / F
6. Charles is John's driver. T / F
7. Mary's mother died when she was a baby. T / F
8. In the end, Mary decided to stay in London. T / F

C. Choose the best answer for each question.

1. John Pearson wanted ___________.
   a. Katy to come to London because she would like it
   b. Mary to come and live in London with him
   c. Mary to learn design in Seattle

2. Katy __________.

a. was excited about being in London

b. did not see any sights in London

c. thought London was boring

3. Mary __________.

a. wasn't nervous about meeting John for the first time

b. didn't take Aunt Lucy's advice

c. was angry with John for leaving her mother

4. Isabel __________.

a. married John when she was very young

b. married Larry and then John

c. left Mary when she was very young

5. Mary's early life __________.

a. was a very happy one because she had everything

b. was hard because she and her mother had little money

c. was troubled because she was sick all the time

Answer Key

A:
1. Lucy; **2.** Isabel; **3.** John; **4.** Harry; **5.** Mary; **6.** Katy

B:
1. T; **2.** T; **3.** T; **4.** T; **5.** T; **6.** T; **7.** F; **8.** F

C:
1. b; **2.** a; **3.** c; **4.** a; **5.** b

Background Reading:

Spotlight on . . . Researching your family tree

A family tree provides information about members of your family, like your mother, father, brother(s), sister(s), grandparents, aunts, uncles, and cousins. This information might be about where they live, their jobs, who they married, and so on.

The information for a family tree can be found in photos, family stories, diaries, and family records, such as certificates of birth, death, and marriage. Many people know about their closest family, but little about their ancestors—the people who lived before them.

There are many ways to find out about your family history:

- Interview everyone in your family about their past—they will probably be happy to talk to you. What stories can they remember?
- Ask family members for copies of photos, certificates, school records, and any information that can help you find out about where your ancestors are from and when they lived.
- Go to the local library and ask them to help you search their records of births, deaths, and marriages. You might find information on your ancestors. Most countries have databases of information going back hundreds of years.
- Search online databases to find long-lost family members or information about your ancestors.

When you are collecting information, it's important to keep accurate notes (write things down, videotape or record voices) so you can find out what information is true and what is just a "story."

Think About It

1. What do you know about your family tree?
2. Which three ways would you choose to research your family tree? How would you record it for your own children and their children?

Glossary

check	(*n.*)	A check is a piece of paper issued by a bank that you sign and give to someone when you promise to pay them money.
comfortable	(*adj.*)	If a chair or room is comfortable, it feels good to be in.
dorm	(*n.*)	A dorm at university is a special building with many bedrooms where students live away from their families.
hug	(*n.* & *v.*)	When you hug someone, you put your arms around him or her to show affection.
leather	(*n.*)	Shoes can be made of animal skin called leather.
luxurious	(*adj.*)	If an apartment is luxurious, it has many expensive things in it.
moment	(*n.*)	A moment is a short period of time—usually a few seconds.
nod	(*n.* & *v.*)	When you nod, you move your head up and down to say yes.
palace	(*n.*)	A palace is a building where kings and queens live.
pregnant	(*adj.*)	If you are pregnant, you are carrying a baby inside you.
servant	(*n.*)	A servant is someone whom you pay to help cook or clean in your home.
shake (shook)	(*v.*)	You shake hands with someone when you greet each other.

spring break	(*n.*)	Spring break at university is vacation time.
stepdad	(*n.*)	Your stepdad is the husband of your mother but not your natural father.
tightly	(*adv.*)	If you hold something tightly, you hold it firmly in your hands.
untidy	(*adj.*)	If you look untidy, you wear your clothes badly and don't even comb your hair.